BACKPACKER

Outdoor
Survival

BACKPACKER.

Outdoor
Survival

SKILLS TO SURVIVE AND
STAY ALIVE

Molly Absolon

Photographs by Dave Anderson

FALCONGUIDES

GUILFORD, CONNECTICUT
HELENA, MONTANA

AN IMPRINT OF GLOBE PEQUOT PRESS

FALCONGUIDES®

Copyright © 2010 by Morris Book Publishing, LLC

Backpacker is a registered trademark of Cruz Bay Publishing, Inc.

FalconGuides is an imprint of Globe Pequot Press.

Falcon, FalconGuides, and Outfit Your Mind are registered trademarks of Morris
Book Publishing, LLC.

Text design by Sheryl P. Kober
Page layout by Melissa Evarts

Library of Congress Cataloging-in-Publication Data
Absolon, Molly.
 Backpacker magazine's outdoor survival : skills to survive and stay alive / Molly
Absolon.
    p. cm. — (Falconguides)
 Includes bibliographical references and index.
 ISBN 978-0-7627-5652-0 (alk. paper)
 1. Wilderness survival. 2. Outdoor life. I. Backpacker. II. Title. III. Title: Outdoor
survival.
 GV200.5.A29 2010
 613.6'9—dc22

                                                                    2009046679
Printed in the United States of America

10 9 8 7 6 5 4

Contents

Planning ahead is one way to avoid survival situations.

Introduction
Outdoor Survival

I stared at the dead tree in disbelief. How had I ended up back here? Maybe it was a different tree. But I knew I was deluding myself. There was no mistaking the fingerlike grey branches of this particular tree. Somehow I'd circled back on myself. I tried to retrace my steps, to get back onto the ridge that led north toward our cabin, but I kept finding myself homing in on the tree. It was as if it had some pull on me, some siren song that kept luring me back. By now I was so confused I had no idea which way was which.

The sky was overcast, obscuring the sun. I knew that the mountains trended north-south, but I did not know if I was facing one way or the other. I knew that roads paralleled the ridge on both sides, so if I went down, I would hit one regardless of which side of the mountain I descended. That seemed like my only alternative. Time to go down. I started moving quickly, fighting to stay calm. I was fine and could spend the night out if necessary, but it was hard to still my racing heart. I wanted to figure out where I was immediately. I wanted to be found.

WHEN THINGS GO WRONG

I was a professional outdoor educator at the time I found myself disoriented on top of North Fork Mountain in eastern West Virginia. I'd spent years leading groups in the wilderness and was pretty cocky about my skill and sense of direction, so it was humbling to find myself so completely and utterly confused on what had started as a short afternoon walk. Unfortunately, most backcountry incidents start out just like mine: A casual stroll or easy trip turns into an epic when you make a wrong turn, fall and get hurt, or are trapped in a storm.

My personal experience that afternoon did not escalate to a level where I'd call it a survival situation, but it might easily have led me to spend the night out. I was assisted by knowing a few tricks that helped me get out of the predicament with little more than a wounded ego. This book is about helping you put together your own bag of tricks, so when the unexpected happens, you can take care of yourself and stay healthy and safe—or at least survive—until help arrives.

WHAT DOES OUTDOOR SURVIVAL MEAN?

Wilderness or outdoor survival conjures up images of building fires using bow drills and shelters from pine boughs, of collecting water drop by drop in a solar still, and gathering food by harvesting wild edible plants or killing small rodents in deadfall traps. These skills—also called primitive-living skills—are interesting to know and challenging to perfect but have little real relevance for most backcountry travelers, even those facing a so-called survival situation.

According to the dictionary, survival simply means "to live through something." The word "something" is vague, but when associated with survival, it usually means an ordeal that tests one's fortitude and knowledge. You survive trials and tribulations, emergencies, tragedies, scary situations. So outdoor survival means living through some difficult challenge in the wilderness, where you cannot call 911 for help and you may be forced to fend for yourself for hours, even days.

Most modern outdoor survival situations result from human errors: You get lost, injured, or in over your head. The focus of this book is on understanding how to avoid these errors and how to minimize their negative effects when avoidance fails. Using a bow drill to light a fire is a cool trick, but when you are stuck out overnight, you are really better off having a lighter safely bagged in plastic and stored in your pocket to get a blaze going quickly. Likewise, knowing that you can eat cattails can be fun and may add some variety and flavor to your backcountry meals, but when you are tired, hungry, and lost in the wilderness, your tummy rumblings will be satiated more readily by pulling an energy bar or chunk of cheese out of your pack rather than by trying to locate a wild plant to eat.

The best possible way to survive an outdoor emergency is to avoid one, and you can avoid many by being prepared and knowledgeable. Before you leave home, you begin the process by packing the appropriate gear, writing a travel plan, anticipating potential hazards or obstacles, making sure you are properly trained, and devising contingency plans. Once you are on your trip, you are constantly on the alert for hazards and take care to make sure your entire team is rested and well cared for to prevent making errors in judgment due to fatigue or injury.

That said, no one is perfect, and it is likely that you may run into trouble at some point if you spend a lot of time in the wilderness. For those times it helps to be ready both mentally and physically.

In this book we outline the steps you should take before you go on your trip so you are prepared; we also identify tricks you can use during your trip to avoid preventable mistakes. Finally, for when things do go awry, we provide you with techniques to help you stay comfortable, calm, and healthy until help arrives.

Chapter One
Preparation

BEFORE YOU GO: PLANNING AHEAD

The first step to avoiding a survival situation is choosing a trip that is appropriate for your skill level. Too often people get into trouble because they underestimate the challenge of their route or overestimate their individual capabilities. Be honest with yourself and with your teammates. If you have never tied into a rope before, you should not have your first experience doing so on a 12,000-foot mountain deep in the wilderness. If you haven't hiked more than a mile in your life, planning to cover 20 in two days on your first trip out is unrealistic.

Take time in town to evaluate your team's abilities so you can choose a trip that will be appropriate for all.

Self-Assessment

To help evaluate the appropriateness of your objective, each member of your team should consider the following questions:

a. What kind of physical condition are you in? Do you work out? If so, for how long? Have you hiked with a pack on? What kind of mileage have you hiked in a day?

b. Have you done a trip of this sort before? If so, what, if anything, is different about this particular plan? If not, do you have any relevant experience that might help you evaluate your potential performance?

c. What skills will the trip demand? How do you rate your competency at these skills? Do you need further training?

d. Does anyone on the trip have first-aid training?

Once everyone on your trip has evaluated him- or herself, you are ready to pool your data and make a plan.

Physical Conditioning

Wilderness trips can be casual—you may ride horses into the mountains and lounge around for five days while a cook prepares meals for you—or you can plan to hike 20 miles or more a day to traverse an entire range. You need to be realistic about how the demands of the trip you are considering align with the reality of your physical ability. Twenty minutes on the treadmill three times a week doesn't really equate well with hiking uphill for five hours with thirty-five pounds on your back.

If you have the time to train for your trip (you'll need a few weeks to really harden your body), do.

A little training will help you enjoy your trip more and may prevent accidents due to fatigue.

Your best bet is to load up a backpack and go hiking. Start slowly and build up time and distance as your body gets used to the weight and motion. If you do not have access to a place to take day hikes, load up a pack and get on the stair climber at your local gym. People may look at you strangely, but there's nothing like training specifically for an activity to ensure that you'll be in shape when you begin the trip.

What does physical conditioning have to do with outdoor survival? A lot, really. If you are out of shape, you are more likely to get injured or become sick. Tired people fall, make bad decisions, stop paying attention to their surroundings, and end up disoriented and lost. Also, if you are miserable, you'll have a lousy time, so why go into the mountains attempting something that is way over your head? Be realistic. Choose an objective that is appropriate for you and for your team.

Experience

Do your research and make sure you know what kind of hazards you may encounter during your trip. Be honest about your experience. It is appropriate to push yourself—you never develop your skills if you don't try something new every now and then—but it is stupid to put yourself into a situation for which you have no training or knowledge. For a basic backpacking trip, the skills required are rudimentary: you must be able to keep yourself warm, dry, fed, and found.

Many outing clubs and wilderness adventure schools offer classes on basic outdoor skills.

Depending on your route, you should include more advanced skills such as being able to cross rivers and read maps or specialized techniques for travel over rock, snow, or ice.

If you are a novice to the outdoors, consider taking a class or finding someone to come along on your trip who is more experienced. Read some books, practice skills at home, hire a guide, join a club. There are all sorts of ways to gain skills without bumbling your way blindly into a bad situation.

Team Composition

Before you head out on your trip, take a moment to sit down with your companions to talk about what you want from the experience. Shared values and desires are critical to ensuring that your team is well functioning and that you have a good time out there. You should be aligned in terms of how hard you want to work, how much risk you are willing to accept, and what you want to achieve. Dysfunctional teams make mistakes and tend to fall apart, which lead to discord and fragmentation.

Choose an Appropriate Trip

With the information you have gathered, you are now prepared to choose a trip that is appropriate for your skill level, your physical conditioning, and your personal goals and objectives. Information on trips can be garnered from any number of places: guidebooks, magazines, the Internet, local outing clubs, guides and outfitters, and outdoor shops are all great places to find out about trips of all levels of difficulty, distance, length, and location.

EQUIPMENT

Many backcountry emergencies result from people being poorly equipped to meet conditions. Backpackers succumb to hypothermia because they fail to bring appropriate clothing. Day hikers forget their maps and end up lost. Proper equipment is critical to navigating through and living comfortably in the outdoors. Proper equipment is also essential to dealing with emergencies.

Research the area you plan to visit to determine the gear you will need to be safe and comfortable.

Coming Up with an Equipment List

It can be daunting to pack for your first wilderness adventure. You want to make sure you have enough, but not too much gear, because you don't want to carry sixty pounds on your back just to make sure you are ready for any and every potential need. Try to carry gear that can serve multiple functions: A water bottle can be your coffee cup; a bandanna a washcloth, hair band, or sunshade. Make detailed lists, and note what you do and do not use so that on future trips you can fine-tune the packing.

I like to divide my gear lists into personal stuff and group gear. Personal equipment includes clothes, toiletries, sleeping stuff, and so forth. Group gear is everything you will share: shelters, cooking

It can snow almost every month of the year in the mountains, so bring layers of clothing that can be added and subtracted as weather conditions change.

equipment, first-aid supplies, and technical tools such as a climbing rack.

Your gear will be dictated by the following considerations:

1. Length of trip

2. Elevation, season, weather

3. Specific goals (climbing, skiing, fishing, birding, etc.)

BASIC GEAR LIST

Personal Gear

1. Upper body layers (base layer, insulating layer(s), and one T-shirt made from polyester or wool; save cotton for trips in hot, dry climates)
2. Lower body layers (base layer, insulating layer, and one optional pair of shorts made from polyester or wool)
3. Raincoat and pants (can be used as wind gear in winter conditions)
4. Breathable wind gear (top and bottom)
5. Warm hat, sun hat
6. Gloves or mittens, socks
7. Hiking shoes, camp shoes (optional)
8. Eating utensils (bowl, spoon, water bottle, lighter)
9. Sleeping bag and pad
10. Toiletries, bug repellent, sunscreen
11. Backpack
12. Water treatment (filter, halogens, etc)

Group Gear

1. Cooking gear (stove, 1–2 pots, channel-lock pliers, water container, spatula or serving spoon, frying pan [optional])
2. Shelter (tent or fly to hold all participants)
3. Spade for digging catholes, toilet paper, trash bag
4. First-aid kit
5. Hand sanitizer or soap
6. Maps, compass, GPS (optional)
7. Communication device (cell or satellite phone, SPOT tracking devices, etc.)

Emergency Gear

In many books you'll see a list of ten essentials, or emergency gear you should have on your person at all times. If you are carrying a full backpack and are prepared to be out for a few days, there is no need to carry extra emergency gear. You should have everything you require to be comfortable available in your backpack. But there is one item many experienced outdoorspeople advocate carrying separately: a lighter in a plastic bag. With a lighter in your pocket you can start a fire to stay warm if something happens; for example, you get lost going to the bathroom near camp or your pack falls in the river and floats downstream. In these kinds of situations, your lighter turns into essential emergency gear.

For day hikes into the mountains or when you leave your camp for a few hours, it does behoove you to carry a few essentials in a small pack just in case the weather changes or you are out longer than anticipated. These include:

>> Extra layer
>> Warm hat
>> Rain jacket
>> Water and water-treatment capability
>> Snack
>> First-aid kit
>> Lighter

A hat provides a lot of warmth for very little weight.

Just remember, carrying emergency gear does not prevent emergencies. Your best weapons in the outdoors are your preparation, common sense, and ability to think clearly under pressure. With these things, you can survive almost anything.

Know Your Gear

Search and rescue professionals are constantly going out to look for lost people who are carrying maps and GPSs but don't know how to use them. It doesn't help to have all the right gear in your backpack if you can't operate it. Take time to learn how to use your equipment before you leave home: Light your stove, set up your tent, practice using your GPS in conjunction with a map. If necessary, seek training to ensure your competency.

Have a more experienced friend help you learn how to use your gear if you are a novice.

With the right equipment, camping can be comfortable and relaxing.

You should also avoid going out on long trips to isolated places with untried gear. Make sure the equipment you bring along does what it is supposed to do. If you haven't used a particular brand of tent or stove, ask around or read reviews on the Internet to ensure that you've chosen a model that will work for your purposes.

If you are using old gear, pull it out of storage and check to make sure it is in good repair before leaving. Carry a repair kit so you have the tools you need to fix your gear if something breaks down—if your stove gets clogged or a tent is torn in a windstorm, for instance.

CONTINGENCY PLANS: PLANNING FOR THE WORST

Competent wilderness travelers are constantly asking themselves "what if" when traveling through the back-country, but the questioning should begin at home. Emergency planning ensures that you are prepared for the unexpected, that people know where and when to look for you, and that your actions are rational and predictable in spite of the emotional trauma associated with any kind of emergency situation.

Here are the steps you need to take before you leave home:

a.   Research outside resources.

 »   Where is the nearest telephone or do cell phones work where you are traveling? Will you carry a cell phone or other emergency communication device (satellite phone or personal locating beacon)?

 »   What agency do you contact for help in an emergency situation (National Park Service, local sheriff's department, Bureau of Land Management, United States Forest Service, and so on)?

 »   What are the logical "escape routes" out of the wilderness (e.g., do the rivers flow out to civilization? Can you reasonably follow them?)

 »   Are there any locations where you may be able to find help, such as an outfitter camp, a

In the continental United States, you can be confident that all rivers eventually will take you to civilization if you follow them downstream, but it may take you a while to get there.

ranger cabin, or a popular destination where you are likely to encounter other campers?

b. Create a detailed itinerary.

» Write out your trip plan, with camping spots, dates, and travel routes identified. Include possible alternatives, potential obstacles, and contingency plans in case you are unable to complete your desired route.

» Identify an approximate end time when you expect to be home, and a second "freak" time—a time when you want people to start looking for you.

» Explain what your action plan is should an emergency occur.

» Outline the equipment and resources you and your team have available.

» Leave a copy of the itinerary with a trusted friend and on the dashboard of any vehicle left at the trailhead.

c. Check in with land management agencies.

» Secure permits for camping (if needed).

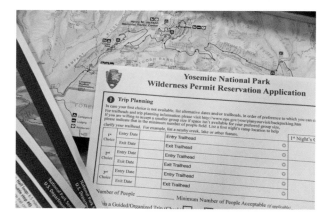

- » Investigate potential hazards or obstacles that could affect your plan (bridges out, landslides, high water, and so forth).
- » Consider leaving an itinerary with the permitting agency.
d. Look into weather conditions.
- » Check into long-term forecasts for the area you are traveling.
- » Gather information on potential weather extremes.

Chapter Two
When Things Go Awry

Regardless of all our planning and training, there will be times when things do not go as planned. Accidents happen, you get lost or separated from your party, someone falls ill, or you misjudge a hazard and end up in trouble far from help. Now's the time to breathe deeply and come up with a plan to get yourself out of trouble.

Sometimes all your preparation comes to naught. Dense forest, off-trail travel, overcast skies can all cause you to become disoriented or lost.

LOST

One of the leading reasons local search-and-rescue teams are called into action is to find lost hikers. It happens every summer all over the country: Hikers fail to show up at a designated meeting place on time; someone wanders off to relieve him- or herself, gets disoriented, and doesn't return to camp; or people don't know how to read their map or GPS and end up miles from where they planned. Getting turned around in the wilderness is actually pretty easy to do; the trickier skill is, knowing where you are at all times.

WAYS TO STAY FOUND

1.   **Pay attention.** As you walk, take time to look around and make note of the landmarks you pass. Orient yourself to the landscape. Do the mountains trend north-south? Are there any major topographical features that can keep you clued in to the cardinal directions? For example, say you are hiking in view of Mount Rainer. Are you to the east, west, north, or south of the mountain? It's unlikely that orientation will change unless you are hiking very long distances, so you can always look at the peak to get an overall sense of which way is which. Of course, this technique is not very

Take advantage of high points and open terrain to get oriented to the surrounding landscape and familiar with obvious landmarks.

helpful when clouds obscure your land-marks, but on clear days it's a great way for you to place yourself in the landscape.

The sun can also help you get a sense of the cardinal directions. Make note of where it rises, watch how it tracks its way across the sky, and notice where it sets. If you check your watch at the same time,

you'll be able to get a sense of time and direction by the sun.

Notice how things look as you move along. Verbalize the shape of the surrounding hills, identify places on your map, and look over your shoulder to get a view from another perspective. Don't keep moving forward if the landscape you see around you is not matching what you expected from reading your map. Your map will tell you if you will be traveling upstream or downstream; gaining or losing elevation; or moving above treeline, in a canyon, or out on a flat plain. If things aren't matching up, you need to figure out why.

2. **Pick out handrails and landings.** Handrails serve as guides, helping you follow a path. In the outdoors, handrails are natural features such as a long ridge or river that acts as a barrier, keeping you on the correct line of travel. For example, your handrail may be a river that you will be following for several miles along its northern bank. That means that if you are traveling west the river should always be on your left side. If suddenly the river disappears or you find it has magically switched to your

right side, you should be clued in to the fact that something has gone wrong.

Landings are places where things change—as landings on a staircase are places to pause and change direction. In the backcountry a landing may be a trail junction, a river crossing, or perhaps a mountain pass. Once you encounter that landing, your

It's hard to get lost when natural features such as these valley walls act as handrails confining you to a specific path.

It can be easy to lose track of where you are when pounding down a trail. Make sure to continue to pay attention to your surroundings to avoid missing key landmarks or trail junctions.

handrails will change. A river may switch sides or you may leave it altogether. You may find yourself traveling downhill after climbing for hours to reach a pass.

Pick out your handrails and landings in the morning before you start hiking. Make note of when you expect to reach specific points along your route. If you thought you'd cross a river at noon and two hours later you're still walking with no sign of water, you probably need to stop and look at your map.

3. **Look at the landscape *before* consulting your map.** If you have been hiking for several hours and your feet and back are getting sore, it can be very easy to look at your map and decide you are someplace close to your destination. You can usually convince yourself that you've hiked farther than you have; and while you thought a mountain landmark was going to be bigger, with a little imagination you can usually make yourself believe it is that rounded knob in front of you, especially if that means you are less than a mile from camp. The phenomenon of making the map fit the land is not purely a habit of beginners. Most of us start to smell the barn when our legs are tired.

To avoid falling into this trap, your best bet is to pinpoint a few key points in the landscape around you before opening your map. These points need to be obvious features that you'll be able to identify on the map, such as the inlet or outlet of a lake, a large meadow with a river meandering through it, a low pass between distant peaks, or a prominent mountain. Usually, it's best to choose a couple of different landmarks to help narrow down your options. Once you've looked around, pull out the map and locate your landmarks. Only after you've found those points is it worth trying to home in on your specific location.

4. **Keep track of time.** Make note of when you leave camp and what time you pass obvious terrain features. This will give you a sense of how fast you are moving and when you should expect to arrive at your destination or a specific spot. Most of us travel at about 3 miles per hour on relatively level trails carrying a light load. Add some elevation gain in, and you can expect to slow down. If you add an extra mile per 1,000 feet gained, you'll get a good approximation of your speed. Off-trail travel is usually slower. Regardless, every party moves at its own pace, so you'll want to pay attention at the start of your trip to get a better sense of what formula works for you.

   Travel speed is useful primarily because it can serve as a gauge. If you calculated that you should reach your camp by 3 p.m. and you find yourself hiking at 5 with no end in sight, it may be that you've gone astray. If you are way overdue and there's no logical explanation for your tardiness (such as a three-hour nap at lunch), stop and reevaluate. You may have made a wrong turn hours ago.

5. **Stay together while hiking.** You don't have to be right next to your teammates at all times, but you do want to be sure you have a system for communicating should the need arise. You may decide that means you always have a designated leader out front and someone else bringing up the rear; you may have a rule that no one gets out of view; or you may decide that you will rendezvous at any decision point you encounter, such as a trail junction or river crossing. The key is to make sure that you do not become separated if something happens: a member of your party is injured, someone is uncomfortable crossing a stream, or part of the group feels too tired to make your destination. In and of themselves, none of these

Stay with your group or have a plan for meeting up if you decide to hike at your own pace. Separated hikers often end up lost hikers because of miscommunication and misunderstanding.

scenarios is particularly dangerous, but if half of your group journeys forward blithely, oblivious to the difficulties faced by the others, you may end up miles apart before you know it.

6. **Know your campsite.** Take a few moments while you are setting up camp to familiarize yourself with your surroundings, especially if your camp is hidden in the trees and hard to see from a distance. Locate some landmarks that will help you home in on the site, so if you wander away to get water, go to the bathroom, or take a hike, you will have some markers to lure you back home. These markers may be a specific boulder, a unique tree, a trail junction, or a waterway: anything you can recognize from all directions.

You may also want to follow these guidelines if you set your pack down and leave it for a few minutes while hiking. It can be surprisingly hard to find a backpack lying in the woods, so take a moment to look around before you leave. That helps ensure you know where to look when you finish your business.

7. **Know how to use your navigational tools.** You can carry a state-of-the-art GPS and know exactly what your coordinates are at

all times, but unless you can translate that information to a map, you can still be lost. Modern tools make staying found easier, but only if you know how to use them. Practice reading your map and using a compass or GPS at home. Seek instruction or assistance from someone who knows more than you if you find yourself confused.

LOST OR CONFUSED?

In spite of everything, most people who spend a lot of time in the wilderness have been disoriented or flat-out lost at some point in their career. The land of 39-foot hills where the map's contour intervals are 40 feet; dense forests where you can see no farther than the next tree; and wide-open terrain without any distinguishing features are all notoriously difficult to navigate through and, therefore, easy to become lost in.

So, what do you do? First and foremost, don't panic. Stop, breathe, and evaluate your situation. Take off your backpack; sit down. As the legendary mountaineer and founder of the National Outdoor Leadership School, Paul Petzoldt, used to say, "Stop and smoke a cigarette." The point is, slow down for a minute. All too often the first thing people do when they realize they are lost is to start moving rapidly back in the direction they think they came from, and before you know it, they have wandered even farther astray. Nothing is going to happen to you in the next few moments, so settle down and come up with a plan.

1. **Retrace your steps in your mind.** Can you backtrack? Do you know where you came from? If it's just a matter of heading back down the trail, by all means, retrace your steps until you are back at a place you recognize, and start over.

2. **Find a high point from which to observe your location.** Is there a nearby hill or open area where you can get a view of your surroundings? Look for major rivers, signs of humans, or recognizable landforms.

Seek out a high point to get a view.

3. **Scout the area to look for recognizable features.** If you can't get to a viewpoint, you can consider scouting around to see if you can find something that will help you get oriented. The trick to scouting is *not* to get separated from your group or gear in the process. Scout in pairs, limit the duration of your exploration, and make sure you can retrace your steps and find your group and gear.

SO YOU ARE LOST: DO YOU STAY OR DO YOU GO?

You've probably heard the old adage: Don't move when you get lost. In fact, if you are a parent, it is likely you've given your child this ultimatum. And often, staying put is the best advice, but not always. To decide if you are better off sitting tight or moving, ask yourself:

» How long will it be before people notice your absence and come looking for you?
» Can you safely stay out overnight or longer waiting for help?
» Do you have shelter? Clothing? Water, food, and a source of heat?
» What is the weather doing?
» Is there a logical path to help?

You should attempt to walk out if one or more of these variables is true:

» The area you are in is unsafe.
» Bad weather is approaching, and you have no shelter.
» Nobody knows you are missing and won't notice for days, so a search is unlikely to be launched anytime soon.
» You have no way to communicate, and you are someplace where a signal—such as a smoky fire or flashing mirror—is unlikely to be noticed.

If you decide to stay put, make yourself comfortable. It may be a while before help arrives.

If you know that people are going to miss you and come looking soon, your best bet is to find an obvious place and stay put until you are found. This strategy is especially true if you get separated from your group. Make noise, build a fire, try to be obvious, but don't start moving until one of the factors listed on the previous page begins to come into play.

Guidelines for Walking Out

If you determine no one is going to come looking for you and your best bet is to attempt to walk to safety, it helps to follow some basic rules of thumb to maximize your chances of being found:

1. **Attempt to hike to a road.** Roads lead to towns, farms, houses, people, so if you can get yourself on a road, eventually you should be able to track down someone who can help you out. In the mountains all streams flow out to the flats, and unless you are near the ocean, sooner or later these streams will be crossed by a road. So start by following rivers downstream—stick to the bigger drainages and keep heading down; eventually you will come to some man-made feature. Trails will likewise take you to roads or towns at some point, so pick the direction that seems to be heading away from the mountains and start walking.

If you have no way to write a message, leave obvious signs that indicate which way you are traveling.

In due course you will come to some help, at least in the continental United States. It may take you a while, but in today's world, you will find people.

2. **Leave notes in obvious places.** Let searchers know of your intentions by leaving notes—or in the absence of paper and writing utensils, some kind of sign—at trail junctions, on the edge of meadows, or by other noticeable landmarks. Use a bright bandanna or something that will catch people's eyes to identify the mark.

Guidelines for Staying Put

Whether you are moving or staying put, your first goal is to make yourself noticeable. So when you stop moving for the day, and whenever you decide to remain in one location and wait for rescue, take time to make some kind of signal to help searchers see you. It can be surprisingly difficult to see a tent or hiker from the air, so use mirrors, smoke, patterns, and sound to make yourself as obvious as possible.

Finally, make yourself comfortable. If you are really, truly lost, it may take hours, even days before you are located, so take time to make a comfortable camp where you will be protected from the elements. Improvise a shelter, build a fire, and stay hydrated. Look at Chapter Four for details.

Effective Signaling Techniques

» Mirrors or shiny objects

Aircraft can often see the flash of a mirror easier than other signaling techniques.

» Smoky fires during the day, blazing ones at night

In the day, use green, wet wood to make a smoky fire most easily seen by searching aircraft. At night, use dry wood to create a bright blaze, again most easily seen by searching aircraft.

» Geometric patterns, bright objects

Regular geometric shapes like squares are not found in nature so they stand out. Use brightly colored clothing or other materials to create large shapes in open spaces to attract the attention of aircraft.

» Noise: Yelling, whistle, banging pots

Make noise to attract the attention of searchers. The sound of banging pots or a whistle carry farther than your voice.

IF YOU NEED TO LOOK FOR SOMEONE ELSE

You may not be the one lost; it may be another member of your party who goes out fishing and fails to return. Before you run for the roadhead to call out the local search-and-rescue squad, it's worth conducting a search on your own, especially if you are traveling with a large group. The key is to be systematic in your searching.

Come Up with a Plan

Gather information first:

» Identify the missing person's last known location and time.
» Discuss the missing person's personality traits. Is he or she likely to panic and move, or will this person stay put? How reliable is this person?
» Brainstorm what gear the missing person may have with him or her.

Once you've decided on a plan of action, follow these steps:

1. **Organize search teams.**

» Make sure no one is searching alone.
» Each team should have marked maps and a clear sense of their location and the area they should search.
» Set return times.

Once you realize someone in your party is missing, it is imperative that you search in an organized, methodical way to avoid having someone else get separated.

2. **Do an initial "hasty" search.**

» Send searchers to obvious places: water, trails, and so forth.

» Focus initial searches downhill of the last known point because people tend to trend downhill when traveling.

» Leave notes in obvious places instructing the lost person to sit tight. Recheck these spots regularly.

3. **Do a fine search.**

» When it becomes clear that you are not going to find the missing person easily, you need to shift your efforts into a more detailed "fine" search. At this point, you will probably need to bring in outside help, as fine searches require lots of people power. If you have a phone, call 911 or send runners to the trailhead to seek assistance. Once help arrives, you will probably be required to turn over leadership of the search.

While you wait for assistance to arrive, you can continue searching. Use the following guidelines to help improve your effectiveness and ensure your team is well cared for.

Stay close together when searching to ensure you cover each area thoroughly.

>> Organize your group into search parties of three or more with a designated leader. Give each team a specific area to examine, and designate a length of time to search.

Your time frame will be determined by terrain, number of searchers, resources, and distances, so it may vary anywhere from two hours to six or even eight. Beware of fatigue. Make sure you do not overtax your volunteers and end up with more problems than you began with.

» Individual search teams should spread out in a line, close enough together so they can see and talk to each other as they walk forward. Call the name of the missing person, and listen for responses. Mark the edges of the places you have searched. Note and flag any clues you may have found, but leave them in place. Repeat this process until the entire search area can be cleared (meaning no sign of the person has been located).

» Maintain one leader back in camp to serve as the Incident Commander. This person will keep track of search teams, determine search areas, and devise action plans, as well as make sure everyone is adequately fed and rested.

Chapter Three
Survival Threats

You've tried everything: written travel plans, carried a map, climbed to a high point, left notes, and still you find yourself lost or separated from your group. This is the time you have to "survive" or take care of yourself until help arrives.

WHAT CAN KILL YOU?

When people die in the wilderness, it is usually a result of trauma, drowning, exposure to either cold or heat, or heart attacks. We worry about starvation, but the reality of the matter is that that isn't what is going to get you.

Trauma: According to search-and-rescue databases maintained by the national parks and rescue groups, unroped falls are the number one cause of death in the backcountry. Most result from carelessness—hikers edging too close to an overlook and slipping on gravel, climbing a rock face they shouldn't, or crossing steep snowfields without crampons or an ice ax. Use extra caution in places where falls are possible and would cause grave injury or death, and never climb up anything unless you are certain you can climb back down. This book is not a first-aid manual, so we will not go into detail about how to deal with injuries in the wilderness, but remember, knowing how to deal with an emergency can save lives. Take a basic first-aid course before you head out on a camping trip. You don't want to watch your loved one die because you never learned how to conduct artificial respiration or stop bleeding. Chapter Five will introduce you to a few key first-aid emergencies you should understand before you go camping.

Drowning: Drowning is the number two cause of fatalities in the backcountry. It can happen in all sorts of ways: Hikers fall crossing rivers; canoeists flip their boats in the middle of lakes due to high winds and waves; anglers slip off river banks and tumble into whitewater; and people fall through ice crossing frozen lakes in the spring.

If you plan to travel in the backcountry, you should learn to evaluate water hazards, whether it's a river or an icy lake. Moving water can be pushy, boulders slippery, and footing difficult in mountain streams, and ice can be rotten on alpine lakes, so look for places to cross where a stream's gradient is mellow, the water is smooth, or the river bottom is gravel or sand, and if you plan to cross ice, pick a place where it is thick enough to sustain your weight. Look downstream for hazards. If you were to fall, are you likely to go into raging whitewater or over a waterfall? Or will you be able to swim to safety?

Logs or logjams and boulders can make good dry crossings, but be careful. They are often slippery and can add the risk of a fall from a height to the potential of drowning. Look for broad, dry logs or large flat boulders, and remember, having wet feet is a small price to pay for a safe crossing.

River-crossing techniques vary. Many people like to face upstream with a large stick in front of them to serve as a third point of contact. You can shuffle your feet across the stream and lean into the current this way. It also allows you to backtrack easily if conditions prove more difficult than you anticipated. You may want to have your teammates line up behind you to form a line. This way the front person acts as a kind of human eddy, easing the push of the current on those behind. Other people hold hands in a human chain to provide some stability during a crossing.

Fast-moving water above knee height is often too strong for most people to cross safely. Do not underestimate its power—if you have concerns, look for another place to cross. If you do fall into the river, flip yourself over onto your back, feet facing downstream. Use your arms and hands to keep yourself upright and your feet to push off obstacles such as rocks and boulders as you move with the current. When you see a calm spot, flip over onto your stomach and swim to the side of the river to safety. Many people advocate crossing rivers with the hip belts of their packs unhooked so they can jettison the pack in the event of a fall. You are certainly more agile without your pack, which will make it easier to swim for shore, but a pack can also protect your back and help you float.

If you plan to travel through areas where you anticipate having to cross a lot of big rivers, get out and practice your crossing techniques in a controlled setting. There's nothing like feeling the push of the current against your body to help you gain a healthy respect for the power of water.

Hypo- or hyperthermia: Our bodies do not adapt well to temperature extremes. In cold, wet, or freezing conditions, you can succumb to hypothermia (too little heat) in a matter of hours. Hyperthermia (or heat stroke) can be equally lethal. After dealing with injuries due to trauma, mitigating your exposure to the elements is going to be your number one priority.

Find a way to get out of the elements. If it is cold and wet outside, you need to figure out how to stay relatively warm and dry. If the temperatures are high and the sun is beating down on you, look for a way to get out of the sun or at least rest during the hottest part of the day.

Dehydration exacerbates the problems of both heat and cold stress but is rarely the cause of back-country fatalities. You can go three to five days without water unless temperatures are extremely hot, so while water is important, it is not going to be the first thing that causes you problems in most backcountry situations.

That said, if you are truly lost and far from help, you are going to need water. Dehydration can lead to decreased mental and physical performance and make you more susceptible to injury, heat, and cold. Unfortunately, there are some places where it is not wise to drink the water without purification—places with cattle, farm runoff, sewage, or a heavily used campsite upstream, for example. Here you should probably disinfect your water. But in an emergency, don't worry, drink. Chances are the water is okay, and even if it isn't, it usually takes anywhere from few days up to a couple of weeks before you'll show signs and symptoms of waterborne illnesses. By then you should be home and have access to doctors and medicine if any problem occurs. In the meantime, you'll be better able to function having fluids in your system.

You cannot tell from appearances if water is safe to drink, so your best bet is to treat all water in the wilderness. However, if you are in a survival situation, water treatment is secondary to hydration.

Heart attacks: Statistically, heart attacks are one of the leading causes of fatalities in the backcountry. Middle-aged men who haven't stayed in hiking shape but try to recapture their youthful glory by attacking a big hike or peak climb seem to be the ones most susceptible to this risk. The main way to reduce your exposure is through lifestyle choices: Maintain a healthy weight and a good level of physical fitness; avoid habits that predispose you to problems, such as smoking; make sure your blood pressure is controlled; and watch your exertion levels by choosing activities appropriate for your fitness, age, and ability. And be honest with yourself: Does your profile fit into that of a person at risk for heart attacks? If so, you should be very careful about the type of backcountry trip you tackle.

Hunger: Food is the least of your worries. People can survive weeks without food, so although going hungry can make you uncomfortable—okay, miserable—you will be fine in the short term if you run out of things to eat.

Chapter Four
Survival Skills

FIRES

Jack London's short story "To Build a Fire" is one of the most gripping tales of outdoor adventures of all time. I haven't read it in probably twenty years, but I can still remember the tension building as the man gathers his wood and prepares to light his one match—his only hope for survival—only to have the feeble flame doused by snow falling from the tree above. Fires can be tricky to build in the outdoors: Wet wood, rain, wind, snow, lack of flame—all can make your efforts frustrating or even futile.

Flame

The need for a reliable source of flame is one reason that many people advocate carrying a lighter in a plastic bag in their pocket at all times. If you keep your lighter dry and it has an adequate supply of fluid inside, you don't have to worry about whether you can start a fire in a driving rainstorm with a single match. If you are more of a purist and prefer matches, make sure you carry them in a waterproof container, and again, it's always a good idea to keep them on your body somewhere in case you get separated from your backpack.

Tinder

If you have some kind of flame starter, the key to your success is ensuring that you have sufficient tinder to sustain a flame until bigger sticks have time to catch fire. When it's wet and cold outside, gathering wood can become more difficult. Usually, you just look for dead sticks on the ground, but if it has been raining for a week, that stuff is going to be soggy and slow to light. To find dry wood in these conditions, you need to be a bit more creative. Look around the base of coniferous trees. Often there will be dead branches still attached to the trunk that stay dry in most rain-storms and work well as tinder. Or look under bushes and shrubs; you may find deadwood that is relatively dry here as well.

If you have a knife, you can make your own dry tinder. I've tried a couple of different techniques. One is to take a large dead branch and just whittle away at the sides until you begin to create dry shavings from the protected core inside. You'll need at least three or four cups of shavings—maybe more if the wood is really wet—to get a fire going, so don't stop too soon.

You can also make a kind of "broom twig," where you peel back shavings from a branch with your knife but leave one end attached so you end up with a lot of dry flakes of wood attached to the central stem. These broom twigs make great fire starters.

Wood

In addition to your pile of dry tinder, you'll need an assortment of sticks of varying sizes. Start small—pinky size—and move up to larger pieces. Make sure you have plenty of little stuff, though. If you get impatient and drop a large log on your flickering flame, you will undoubtedly douse it before you've begun. Again, focus your wood gathering under trees, rocks, and shrubs if it is wet out. If the wood has had some kind of protection, it may not be too saturated.

Building Your Fire

I learned how to build a fire in Girl Scouts probably forty years ago. We used to make a central tipi from tiny twigs and surround it with a log cabin (kind of a Lincoln Log-type structure) made from larger sticks. I still use this basic pattern today. The advantage is that it allows adequate airflow and gives some structure to your fire that ensures the wood is touched by flame. Start your tipi with a branched twig stuck into the ground surrounded by a mound of shavings. Lean your twigs against this central pole until you have a cone-shaped structure. Build your log cabin on the outside,

and light the shavings. Once your tipi is burning, lay sticks across the top from side to side of the log cabin, increasing the size of the sticks as your fire gets established. Within a few minutes you should have a cheerful blaze to warm your hands and your spirit.

Technology

If you are lost with your backpack, by all means ignore the previous advice and douse your wood with a little white gas to get it going. This technique may not be the most pure, but it is very effective. You can also place your twigs on a lit stove to get them burning. Be careful, playing with fire is dangerous, and white gas is particularly hazardous. I've seen people fling burning bottles of fuel in a panic, thereby lighting duff and grass in an instant. To prevent such accidents, pour some gas on the wood, recap your fuel bottle, and place it well away from the fire site before you strike a match.

Remember, white gas will not explode. If your fuel bottle does happen to catch fire, place it on the ground, and smother the flames with a metal cook pot.

Ethics

In an emergency situation, your safety preempts environmental concerns. Build a fire if you need to, and don't worry about scorched rocks or fire scars. You should not abuse this privilege by building a raging bonfire anytime your socks get wet, but in a life-threatening scenario, a fire is justified. Ease your conscience next time you go camping by cleaning up dirty campsites and trashed fire rings.

SHELTERS

Getting out of the elements is often critical to survival in the wilderness. In some parts of the world—say, the Colorado Plateau in southeastern Utah—cliffs often form alcoves or overhangs where you can seek shelter and protection from rain, wind, and snow. Other parts of the world are less conducive to an easy hideout, and you may need to improvise a bit to come up with a protected shelter.

Natural Shelters

Overhangs, boulders, and caves can all serve as shelters from the elements, but there are other natural shelters that can fill that function as well. Dense stands of trees with low-hanging limbs often keep much of the rain or snow away. You can also crawl into thick bushes to get some protection. Remember, however, that you are invisible once you burrow down in the trees, so take care to leave some sign of your presence nearby in case searchers visit the area while you are resting.

Tarp

If you have a poncho or a ground cloth, as well as some string, you may be able to rig up a tarp to keep the rain off. Grab a pebble, and place it in the corner of your tarp. Wrap the pebble up like a present and tie your string around it. Do this in each corner to make guylines for your shelter. Then attach the lines to trees or rocks to set up a wind block of sorts. Your best bet is to rig it at a steep angle on the windward side so the tarp serves more like a sloping wall than a flat roof.

Tree-Branch Lean-To

In forested areas you can create a lean-to from dead limbs to serve as a shelter. Gather a bunch of large dead branches—about the size of your arm in diameter and 4 feet long or more. Find a boulder or downed tree, and lean the branches up to create a small cave-like space beneath. Try to overlap the branches, or place grass or leaves in between to fill in the spaces.

Snow Shelters

Snow is a good insulator and can be carved and sculpted into elaborate shelters that are great for keeping the elements at bay. If you are out in the winter or up high enough in the mountains to encounter year-round snow, a shovel is an integral piece of equipment for just this reason. You can build a snow

cave or other form of shelter that protects you from the wind and cold. Temperatures in a snow cave usually hover right around freezing, which will feel balmy if it's below zero outside.

You can still take advantage of snow's insulating properties without a shovel. Your shelter won't be as comfortable, but it will help. Hollow out a shallow trough in the snow with your hands, line the bottom with a sleeping pad, backpack, spare clothes, or pine boughs—anything to keep you off the snow— then climb in and cover yourself with something. Again, you'll need to improvise. Anything can work—a tarp, tree limbs, blocks of snow, even your backpack will help keep you warm.

You can also use tree wells—the moatlike structures that form around the base of trees in the snow— to provide you with some protection from wind and snow. As with a trench shelter, you'll need something to keep you off the ground and to cover you up.

Chapter Five
Basic Wilderness First Aid

This book is not a first-aid manual, and you should seek training if you intend to spend time in the wilderness. That said, there are some basic skills that are critical for everyone planning a trip into the wilderness.

First and foremost is the safety of the rescuer. Too often people compromise their own safety in an effort to save someone else. Before you approach an injured or sick person, stop and survey the scene to determine if it is safe for you to approach. Deciding not to help could be one of the most difficult situations you ever face, but creating two victims helps no one.

INITIAL ASSESSMENT

In any first-aid scenario—illness, injury, mystery—care begins with an initial assessment. You may have heard of the ABCs of first aid—this acronym addresses the immediate threats to life: airway, breathing, circulation, cervical spine. Your first priority is to ensure that your patient's ABCs are stable: that he or she is breathing, and that his or her heart is beating. This is the time you "look, listen, and feel" for breath sounds, heartbeat, bleeding, and other signs of trauma. If any of an individual's ABCs is compromised, you need to stop and fix the problem immediately. No air means you have just minutes before your patient will die; no heartbeat, the same. To address these problems you must have training in cardiopulmonary resuscitation (CPR) and artificial breathing. You must know how to clear an airway and to stop bleeding. You need to know how to avoid adding further damage to a spinal cord injury.

The ABCs have been expanded to include D and E. D stands for disability and clues you in to look for obvious deformities resulting from trauma. E stands for both exposure and environment and serves to remind you to look at or expose the patient's body as you conduct your assessment to ensure you do not miss anything. Environment just reminds you to be aware that the environment may be life threatening in and of itself. Is your patient submerged in freezing cold water or lying in direct sun? Are you both exposed to rockfall or avalanche hazard? These factors may also demand immediate attention.

Stabilize Your Patient

Once you have determined that the ABCDEs are okay, you need to make your patient comfortable. The big difference between wilderness and front-country medicine is the time it takes to get a patient to a hospital. At the very best you may get help in a matter of hours, but it is more likely that you will need to care for an individual for a day or two before you can get him or her out of the backcountry.

Stabilize your patient in a position of comfort. If he can talk to you, let him help you figure out the best position. If he cannot, rest him on his side in case he vomits. Put him on some kind of pad to protect him from the ground; cover him with a sleeping bag or warm clothing. If the patient is conscious and capable of feeding himself, give him food and water. Monitor the individual's vital signs, and go for help. Ideally, you have enough people in your group to allow someone to remain with your patient while others go for help. If there are just two of you, you are faced with a decision. Can you leave your patient to seek aid? Or do you need to stay put to provide care? Some form of communication device such as a personal locator beacon can help in this kind of situation.

SECONDARY SURVEY

After your patient is stable and resting, take time to go through a more thorough history of his illness or injury. The more information you can relay to rescuers, the better. Ask questions about everything: history of the present illness or injury, what your patient ate, when she last had a bowel movement, when the illness began, what her pain is like, whether she has taken any medications or illegal drugs, if she has any chronic illnesses that may have contributed to her

current condition—anything that may help doctors determine what is going on.

You should also conduct a thorough physical exam to make sure you haven't missed anything. Sometimes one injury or problem will mask others, so it's important to double check. Start at your patient's head and move down to her toes. Look, listen, and feel. Be systematic.

Finally, take your patient's pulse and count her breaths. Remember, a normal pulse ranges from sixty to eighty beats per minute, while we breathe between twelve and twenty times per minute. Check skin color and temperature. Ask questions to determine your patient's level of consciousness: name, date, time, what happened? These vital signs—heart rate, breathing rate, skin color and temperature, and level of consciousness—are good ways to monitor your patient over time. Check vital signs regularly, and record your findings. Any changes may indicate a change in your patient's condition.

HYPOTHERMIA

Hypothermia is one of the leading causes of problems, even death, in outdoor survival situations, so having a basic understanding of the illness is critical. You must know the environmental conditions that lead to hypothermia and recognize its signs and symptoms so you can respond should the situation arise.

Simply speaking, hypothermia is a drop in body temperature. Human beings are designed to operate within a limited range of temperatures, and even a few degrees' change on either side of normal can begin to cause problems. Severe changes can be deadly. Any time you find yourself having trouble staying warm and dry, you should be on the lookout for hypothermia, both in yourself and in others.

The first signs of hypothermia are usually shivering, loss of fine motor function (you have trouble zipping up your jacket or tying your shoes), and lethargy. You lose motivation to take care of yourself, preferring to sit around and shiver. As your body cools, these signs become exacerbated, and others join in: changes in personality or levels of consciousness, loss of gross motor functions (inability to walk), irritability, disorientation, strange behavior. At its worst, you lose consciousness. Victims of severe hypothermia are very sick; you can cause heart arrhythmia by moving them too quickly. These people need immediate hospitalization and still may not survive.

Preventing Hypothermia: How Do We Lose Heat?

1. **Radiation:** Our bodies radiate or give off heat as a by-product of metabolism, and exercise—basic living—all the time.

Your head represents approximately 10 percent of your body's surface area, which is a lot of area to lose heat from. Cover up when the temperature starts dropping.

2. **Conduction:** Temperatures want to be equal; that is, if you place your warm bottom on a cold rock, the rock will conduct or pull heat away from you until the two bodies reach equilibrium or the same temperature. Obviously, you cannot generate enough heat to bring a slab of granite to 98.6º Fahrenheit, so you'll be losing a lot of heat to the rock through conduction.

3. **Convection:** Moving air or water displaces the heat that you are radiating from your body and replaces it with cooler air or water.

4. **Evaporation:** When sweat or moisture evaporates off our skin, it cools us down. This is a critical part of our body's temperature regulation capacities, but when in the outdoors, too much sweating can cause excessive heat loss.

How Do You Minimize Heat Loss?

1. **Clothing:** Since humans don't have much hair or any feathers, we rely on our clothing to protect ourselves from the elements. The best technique is to dress in layers that can be added and subtracted easily as temperatures change, because change they will. In the Rocky Mountains it is common for temperatures to fall well below freezing at night

Temperatures are constantly changing in the mountains. Add that to your own changing exertion level, and you'll find you constantly need to add and subtract layers to stay comfortable.

and rise to 70° or higher during the day. These extremes can be even more dramatic in the desert, so you need to be prepared for just about anything.

Think about the ways you lose heat when choosing your clothing. Insulating layers—down or synthetic parkas—help trap your radiant heat loss, as does a hat. Wind layers reduce the effect of convection, and wearing clothing that wicks moisture away from your skin or dries quickly—wool or some kind of synthetic fabric—helps reduce the negative effects of evaporative cooling. (In the desert, where you want to be cool, cotton is best, as it holds moisture and dries slowly.)

2. **Insulation from cold surfaces:** To reduce the effects of conduction on your body, you need to place a barrier between your body and the cold body that wants to steal all your heat. A foam sleeping pad makes a good butt pad, or you can sit on your backpack. In the winter it is helpful to stand on a pad of some kind while you are in camp to keep your feet warmer. If you don't have gear, improvise. Branches, dry grass, pine boughs, extra clothing, anything that will keep you away from the ground will help.

3. **Protection from moving air and water:** Your best bet to reduce your exposure to convection is to remove yourself from the offending environment. Get out of the water as quickly as you can; find a place where you are protected from the wind. Improvise a shelter of some sort, dig a trench in the

snow, climb into a tree well, find an over-hang, get behind a rock—anything that protects you from the wind will help.

In hot climates the wind can be cooling, but it can also accelerate water loss. Use your judgment. I usually prefer to seek shelter from the wind and the sun in the desert. I don't think the cooling properties of moving hot air outweigh the discomfort of its drying effect.

4. **Avoid excessive sweating:** If you are more concerned with cold than heat, you want to try to minimize your sweating. Once you drench your clothes with sweat, you have to dry them again somehow. Usually, that will be your body's job, and it takes a lot of energy (read heat) to dry a soaking-wet T-shirt. In cold temperatures try to moderate your exercise so you don't overheat. Make sure you are wearing the minimum amount of clothing necessary to stay comfortable without sweating too much.

5. **Build a fire for warmth:** If you've been trained to be a low-impact camper, you've been told to minimize the use of fires, keep them small, and only use wood that is on the ground. In an emergency these rules go out the window. But don't abuse the

privilege. If you are not really in danger, there is no need to build a bonfire.

Nonetheless, if you are freezing and don't have any shelter or extra clothing, by all means, build a big fire. It can serve as both a signal for searchers and a way to help you stay comfortable if temperatures drop below freezing. Just take care not to start a wildfire.

Treatment

In the initial phases of hypothermia, the best thing to do is get your muscles moving to generate heat. Do fifty jumping jacks, go for a run up a hill, dance around, get your heart rate up, and you'll warm up. If your clothes are wet, change into something dry or at least wring out the excess water if you have no spares, and put on a hat and dry socks. Start up the stove, and have a warm drink. Eat a sugary snack. Usually, if you catch your chill quickly enough, these measures will be enough to take care of the problem.

If, you begin to see more severe symptoms of hypothermia in your patient or yourself, you need to take dramatic action. The old treatment was to put the hypothermic person in a sleeping bag naked with another naked person. The idea was that the hot person would warm the cold one, which is true, but this technique can cause the warm individual to get chilled. Besides, most people probably wouldn't be comfortable getting naked with most of their camping mates. These days people advocate using warm-water bottles against the skin of the hypothermic patient. Place the patient in a sleeping bag with

In the early stages of hypothermia, you need to get out of the cold and into dry clothes. A hot drink and food can also help.

warm-water bottles under his armpits, in his groin area, against the palms of his hands. Make sure the bottles are not so hot that they could cause a burn.

You may want to wrap the sleeping bag in a tarp or tent fly—some kind of waterproof, windproof layer that will trap heat—and make a kind of cocoon around your patient. Cover everything but the individual's face.

If you are successful in warming your patient, remember that he will be exhausted from the experience and may need a few days rest to get back to normal. If your patient is catatonic and unresponsive because of hypothermia, do not attempt to rewarm him in the field. He needs to be in a hospital. Wrap him in a sleeping bag, blanket, or something else that will prevent further heat loss, and seek immediate help.

FROSTBITE

Frostbite, or frozen fingers and toes, is another environmental injury frequently suffered by survivors of outdoor emergencies. Most common on your extremities, frostbite occurs when the liquids in your body freeze. Frostbite can cause serious tissue damage and may lead to amputation in extreme situations.

The first step in preventing frostbite is limiting exposure. Frostbite occurs in temperatures below freezing. Areas with obstructed blood flow—feet confined to tight boots or hands clinging to an ice ax—are

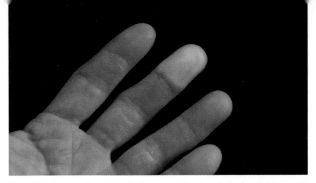

Frostbite leaves the affected area white, hard, and painless until thawed.

particularly susceptible, as are places exposed to the cold, such as your cheeks and nose.

Like a burn, frostbite comes in different depths, affecting various skin layers. Superficial frostbite, or frost nip, is the classic white spot on your cheek on a cold ski day. Usually, all you need to do for frost nip is to cover your face with your hands and blow. The warm air from your breath is enough to get the blood flow back to the tissue. The worst effect of frost nip is normally red and painful skin, similar to that of a sunburn.

As the freezing goes deeper, your signs will worsen. Your extremities may appear wooden, hard, and gray or waxy looking and feel numb. Frozen tissue is painless, so if you can still feel your toes, that's a good sign. It means you don't have frostbite—yet, that is. You need to take care of cold toes before they freeze to minimize the damage. Take your boots off, change your socks, put your cold feet on someone's warm belly—get those toes warm rather than ignore the signs.

If you do get frostbite, you have a decision to make. The treatment is to rewarm the area rapidly in warm water (not so hot that it burns). But if you are in

If you have to walk out to get to help, you may choose not to rewarm a frozen toe or finger. Once frostbite is thawed, the injury is very painful and susceptible to refreezing.

the wilderness and cannot keep your feet warm after they have been thawed, you may be better off keeping the tissue frozen. You may also find that once you rewarm a frozen part, you lose all function because of the pain.

HEAT EXHAUSTION AND HEATSTROKE

Heat injuries are common when temperatures rise and you are exercising in the sun. The most common scenarios include people passing out during marathons or while cutting their grass on a hot August afternoon. Heat exhaustion is usually relatively benign, but heatstroke, which can either follow untreated heat exhaustion or come on suddenly with no warning, is very serious and causes lasting problems or death.

The best treatment for heat injuries is to avoid them. If you know the temperatures are going to be high, alter your schedule to avoid extreme exertion during the heat of the day. Go on a night schedule: Sleep during the day and move at night, or at least take a siesta when temperatures are highest. Make sure that you stay hydrated and that your electrolyte balance is maintained by eating regularly throughout the day. Water without food can lead to a condition called hyponatremia, which is caused by too much water and too few electrolytes. Hyponatremia can be deadly, so be sure that when you drink you also eat. Diluted energy drinks are also helpful in maintaining

Avoid heat injuries by wearing cotton clothes that are easy to ventilate, staying hydrated, and resting during the heat of the day.

your electrolyte balance on hot days when you are working hard.

Signs, Symptoms, Treatment

Hot, flushed skin; profuse sweating; and extreme fatigue usually indicate heat exhaustion. Heatstroke victims may be pale and no longer sweating but not always. The most critical sign of heatstroke is a change in your patient's level of consciousness. She may be irritable, irrational, or confused. She may also pass out.

Heat exhaustion is treated by removing your patient from the offending environment. Get the affected party into the shade and cool her down by placing a wet, cold bandanna on her forehead. Have her drink. Usually, your patient will begin to recover quickly, but it may take a day or two before she feels restored. Heatstroke victims need immediate attention from a doctor. You need to arrange for a helicopter evacuation for these individuals as quickly as possible. In the meantime, get the patient into the shade and begin cooling her with a damp cloth.

ENVIRONMENTAL DANGERS

The wilderness gets its name from its very wildness. Animals are not confined to cages, rocks fall, rivers rage, and mosquitoes buzz. You don't need to be paranoid about these things, just aware of them and knowledgeable about how to minimize your risk.

Wild Animals

Before you head off into a new place, check to see if you need to be concerned about bears or mountain

Bears tend to avoid people unless they associate them with food.

lions. You should also find out if you need to protect your food from rodents, birds, or raccoons. These proverbial camp robbers may not pose a risk to your life, but they can be a nuisance and may steal your food.

Areas with large bear populations often have specific camping guidelines to help prevent encounters. Usually, you must store your food in some kind of bearproof container or hang it high in a tree. The goal is to keep the bears from associating humans with food. Unfortunately, once this happens bears become dangerous and often end up having to be killed by wildlife managers. So proper food storage is critical for both your safety and the safety of the bears.

Mountain lions are not known to be camp robbers, but they do occasionally attack and kill humans. Your best strategy for dealing with mountain lions is

Mountain lions rarely attack large groups of people, so stay together in cougar country.

to know if they are in the area and are causing problems. If alone, you may choose not to go camping someplace if a mountain lion has been on the prowl, or you may decide to go but stay in a large group of people at all times. Most mountain lion attacks have been on individuals.

Bugs

Mosquitoes, ticks, scorpions, bees, and spiders can be annoying, give you the creeps or a nasty sting, and, in some cases, carry disease. Make sure you know if anyone in your group is allergic to bees before you head out. Otherwise, your best bet is to do a little research about what insects you may encounter and what if any measures you can take to manage them. West Nile fever, Lyme disease, Rocky Mountain spotted fever, and other insect-borne diseases can be quite serious, so know what is

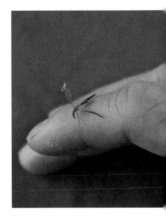

Most bugs are just annoying, but some carry disease. Do tick checks, wear repellent, and cover up so your skin is not exposed to bites or stings.

out there before you go, and be prepared to minimize your exposure. Cover up, wear insect repellent, and avoid traveling during seasons when the bugs are really bad.

Chapter Six

Special Considerations for the Solo Traveler

Risk equals hazard multiplied by consequences. In the backcountry you are often exposed to a variety of hazards—rockfall, weather, moving water, and so forth. The consequences of this exposure can be quite dire, but proper training and experience help you avoid these hazards or mitigate the risk.

The risk of wilderness travel becomes greater when you are alone, largely because the consequences are increased when there is no one to assist you if you get into trouble. Suddenly, a minor inconvenience becomes a major problem, such as a broken ankle deep in the mountains. With your friends such an injury is challenging; you may have to be carried, or someone may need to run for help to move you to safety. Alone, the injury can be life threatening.

Several years ago a solo traveler in the Wind River Mountains of Wyoming became trapped when a boulder rolled and pinned his ankle. The man was unable to move. Search-and-rescue teams searched for him, but by the time he was found, he'd died from thirst, unable to reach a stream that was less than 100 feet away. The tragedy could have been averted if the hiker had been with friends or had stayed on a well-trodden path. That was not his goal, however. He was seeking the solitude of a solo trip. Many people desire this experience, and there is nothing inherently wrong with going out into the woods alone. But solo travelers must recognize that they have narrowed their margin of error by traveling without others to help if things go wrong.

If you choose to go into the mountains by yourself, you must have a heightened awareness of hazards and their consequences. Always play the "what if" game as you make decisions, and remember to consider the fact that you are alone in the equation.

In addition, make sure people know where you are going and when to expect you back. You should carry some communication device. If a cell phone works in the area you plan to visit, carry one. If not, consider investing in some kind of personal locating beacon (PLB). There are a number of different brands of PLBs on the market, such as the SPOT personalized tracker. All send out a signal that enables searchers to locate your position in an emergency. An alternative option is to rent a satellite phone, which enables you to make phone calls from places where cell phones do not work.

Solo travel brings with it some very tangible rewards that are difficult to experience in a group. Alone, you make all your own decisions. You determine where to camp, when to sleep, when to rise, what to eat, and where to go. You decide if you even want to move on any given day. You are surrounded by the sounds and beauty of nature with little to distract you. You are under no pressure to perform or meet another's expectations. The experience of such solitude is rich and for many very compelling. But that freedom has a price: you also have to get yourself out of trouble should it arise.

This book is not meant to dissuade you from experiencing the wilderness on your own if that is your desire. Rather we simply want to remind you to think about the implications of solo travel before you go. Without friends to help, you have very little room for error.

Resources
Education

There are many organizations offering courses on outdoor skills. You can take a refresher class lasting an hour or a semester-long course offering a wide range of skill development. In your community, check out the outfitting stores, guide services, or universities to see what programs are available.

A few of the big outdoor names are:

» The National Outdoor Leadership School, which has been offering wilderness skills development and leadership training in the United States and abroad since 1965.
http://www.nols.edu

» Outward Bound, which also offers a variety of skills training around the world.
http://www.outwardbound.org

» In the northeastern United States, the Appalachian Mountain Club, headquartered in New England, sponsors trips, courses, and employment opportunities in the outdoors for all ages.
http://www.outdoors.org

» In the northwest, the big name is the Mountaineers, a Seattle-based club that provides training in backpacking, climbing, and mountaineering.
http://www.mountaineers.org

FIRST AID

For wilderness travelers, the best first-aid training comes from programs that focus on backcountry first aid. These programs concentrate on long-term care and improvised systems in the absence of immediate access to life support and hospitals. Wilderness Medicine, NOLS Wilderness Medicine Institute (WMI), and Solo all offer wilderness first-aid courses around the country. You can also check with the American Red Cross for first-aid training, but remember, often Red Cross courses will be more frontcountry oriented.

» Wilderness Medicine
http://www.wildernessmedicine.com

» NOLS Wilderness Medicine Institute (WMI)
http://www.nols.edu/wmi/courses/wildfirstaid.shtml

» Solo Schools
http://www.soloschools.com

» American Red Cross
  http://www.redcross.org

GENERAL INFORMATION

» http://gorp.away.com/index.html
» http://www.nps.gov/index.htm
» http://www.fs.fed.us

Index